Too Young To Be Old

The Story of Bertha Pitts Campbell

revised edition by
Pauline S. Hill

authorHOUSE

*Blessings always, Shirley and many thanks for all your support!
Pauline S. Hill
March 2013*

AuthorHouse™
1663 Liberty Drive, Suite 200
Bloomington, IN 47403
www.authorhouse.com
Phone: 1-800-839-8640

©2008 Pauline S. Hill. All rights reserved.

No part of this book may be reproduced, stored in a retrieval system, or transmitted by any means without the written permission of the author.

First published by AuthorHouse 7/9/2008

ISBN: 978-1-4343-9255-8 (sc)

Library of Congress Control Number: 2008905527

Printed in the United States of America
Bloomington, Indiana

This book is printed on acid-free paper.

This Revised Edition is dedicated to:
Sam, Shawn, Sarah, and Nate-Nate Simmons
Bruce and Nigel Williams

David Anderson, Lavern Loud, Thelma & Willie Payne,
Emily & Bob Williams, & Glenda Faye Madison

Members of
Bellevue Alumnae Chapter
Delta Sigma Theta Sorority, Inc.
Bellevue, WA

Members of
Delta Sigma Theta Sorority, Inc., the AME Church,
other civic organizations mentioned in this book
Past, Present, and Future!

Women Everywhere!

Acknowledgements

Without my family, extended family, church family, friends, sorority sisters (sorors), professors and teachers of the past, and our ever-loving God, I could not have completed this Revised Edition of *Too Young to Be Old: the Story of Bertha Pitts Campbell*. I thank each of you for your support as well as for your love.

I acknowledge the diligence of the writers whose works I've read online and in non-online print. I thank you for capturing our history for present and future authors and readers and for leaving a legacy which helps to set straight a history that has not told the experiences of those of us of African descent.

I acknowledge with overwhelming appreciation the following people:

Colleen Sterling, my friend and soror, who has supported and encouraged me from the beginning of this work; Shawn Simmons, my daughter and friend, who edited this edition, and who is always there for her mother; Glenda Faye Madison, my friend and sister, who edited this edition and reminded me to stay the course; and Mona H. Bailey, our 17th National President, Delta Sigma Theta Sorority, who supported this revised work with pictures and the Foreword just as she supported the original edition in 1981. Special appreciation is extended to Sherrilyn Johnson Jordan, friend and soror, who collaborated on the original edition, and who gave her blessings on this revised edition – my prayers remain with you, my sister. Also, thank you to three who shared their opinions of this work – Rev. Ellis H. Casson, Presiding Elder (Retired), Pacific Northwest Conference, A.M. E. Church ; Rev. Carey G. Anderson, senior pastor, First A.M.E., Seattle ; and Kevin P. Henry, Cultural Diversity Coordinator, Bellevue, Washington.

I acknowledge my late parents and my ancestors upon whose shoulders I continue to stand and rely. I acknowledge and thank each person who reads this work! May peace, love, and joy abide for us all and for the world!

Table of Contents

Foreward	xi
Preface	xiii
Prologue	xvii
Chapter 1	1
Chapter 2	3
Chapter 3	13
Chapter 4	19
Chapter 5	22
Chapter 6	29
Chapter 7	34
Chapter 8	38
Chapter 9	53
Chapter 10	55
References	69
About the Author	71

Foreward

Nineteen thirteen was the year Bertha Pitts Campbell along with twenty-one other Black college educated women, banded together and founded Delta Sigma Theta Sorority. Denied membership into white organizations, they did not spend time protesting. They forged their own instrument for change by founding one of the greatest Black women's organizations of all time.

Founding a Black women's sorority did not compromise Bertha Pitts Campbell and the other founders' fervor for ridding the nation of its racist mentality; if anything, their unity in the Delta sisterhood strengthened their resolve. They simply obeyed an injunction, "Go thou and do likewise," in founding an organization whose mission continues to be to work for justice and equality of opportunity for all people.

From her earliest days as an undergraduate at Howard University to her years as an active participant in the affairs of the city of Seattle, Washington, Bertha Pitts Campbell always took her place at the table of leadership to address the needs of the people of the greater Seattle area. She demonstrated love for her sorors and all people and she took pride in their accomplishments. She never compromised truth; she always demanded justice; and she urged others to take the same just stand. She cleaved to love and always murmured exultations of pride.

Too Young to Be Old: the Story of Bertha Pitts Campbell captures the awesome power of an authentic lady whose physical and mental strengths were unparalleled even unto death at nearly 101 years old.

With honor, humility, fond memories and much love, I continue to salute Bertha Adine Pitts Campbell.

        Mona Humphries Bailey
        17th National President
        Delta Sigma Theta Sorority, Inc.

BERTHA ADINE PITTS CAMPBELL

Bertha's Family:
Earl Allen Campbell, Sr., husband
Earl Allen Campbell, Jr., son
Hubbard (HS) Sydney Pitts, father
Ida Butler Pitts, mother
Eliza Butler, grandmother
Charles, Minnie, Tom, and Huey Pitts, siblings

Preface

Revised Edition

It has been twenty-seven years since this work first appeared; even more poignant, it has been eighteen years since the central figure of this work left her earthly home. When *Too Young to Be Old: Bertha Pitts Campbell* was first published in 1981, Bertha Adine Pitts Campbell yet lived, and was ninety-two years old. An ongoing quest for knowledge about the life of one who understood what it meant to be humane, human, and humble for nearly 101 years, drives this revised work.

This easy read, shares the personal story of Bertha Adine Pitts Campbell: as a child growing up with her parents and grandmother, and as a primary, secondary, and college student. It also shares Bertha's career, life as a wife and mother, a public servant in Seattle, Washington, and her life with Delta Sigma Theta Sorority, Inc. When Bertha Pitts Campbell died in 1990, the Sorority had increased from one chapter with 22 members to a membership of 175,000 college-educated women in more than 800 chapters in the United States, and several Republics. At the writing of this Revised Edition in early 2008, the Sorority has a membership of more than 250,000 college-educated women in 950+ alumnae and collegiate chapters located in the United States, the Bahamas, Bermuda, Germany, Tokyo and Okinawa, Japan, Seoul, Korea, and St. Croix and St. Thomas in the U.S. Virgin Islands.

This author believes that the popularity of the Sorority is due largely to the adherence to the founding Christian principles and the continuation of public service work in local area chapters, as well as the national and international leadership of the Sorority and its members.

Pauline S. Hill, author
Renton, Washington
March 2008

Too Young to Be Old

THE STORY OF BERTHA PITTS CAMPBELL

revised edition by
Pauline S. Hill

Prologue

Hubbard Sydney Pitts busied himself with the work that had to be done before his family could start their long journey westward. He called out directions to his wife Ida, and to his first-born, Charles, and as fast as they could finish one task, he would bellow out another. Even Minnie, who only came up to his knees, had to help.

Packing the few worldly possessions posed no problems to Hubbard Sydney, or HS, as he was so fondly called, until he walked out to his adobe-made barn. The way he stoically walked toward the barn made Ida and the children think twice about following him. They stood under the straw-thatched porch of the house and watched him go back and forth from the house to the barn. After several trips, he went into the barn and didn't come out. Ida knew that he would be inside that barn for a long time.

At first, the sorting through his tools and his collections of odds and ends went smoothly and almost rapidly. Then HS came to his scythe, his small but Herculean scythe which was as familiar to him as the hair on the back of his hands.

Hubbard Sydney picked up that scythe carefully and ran his hand alongside the blade, caressing that tool ever so gently, being cautious not to touch the blade for he always kept that blade razor sharp.

So many memories began to tug at his heart, some of which were so powerful, he decided to place the sharp blade on the straw-padded items in the trunk fearing that he'd unintentionally harm himself.

Hubbard Sydney felt that he had made the right decision to move his family away from Winfield, Kansas. After all, what was a man to do when suddenly his livelihood became threatened by an unending drought and when he received prices too low for the few goods he did have to sell?

What was a man to do when money became so very scarce that he could hardly figure out his children's future beyond one year? To provide for his family, wasn't that what a man was for!

The issue did not really become critical in his mind until Ida announced that she was pregnant with their third child. He knew then that the inevitable had finally arrived. He began to conjure up the stories about which he had heard so much: the stories of the mines in Colorado, the precious mines of gold, granite, and coal. There were also the 'mines' of hope, promise, and dreams for his children's future. What would it be like to live near Ida's mother Eliza, who lived in Colorado?

As HS closed the top of the huge, heavy trunk that held his beloved scythe, the lid of tranquility to his heart and mind opened. He had a thought – no, in his mind - he had a plan!

Hubbard Sydney emerged from the barn feeling like he was the old HS again. Relishing his plan as if it had just happened, HS closed the barn behind him, reaching the house after the entire family had gone to bed. He enjoyed the still of the night and moved quietly about the house. He peeked in at the children and snuggled in with his wife, feeling at peace with himself.

As time passed, HS felt free from mind-boggling problems. He was even able to think about whether his third child would be a girl or a boy and would their third child look like him, Ida, or a combination of the two. On June 30, 1889 when their second daughter was born, he thought he noticed that the little girl who looked like him and looked up at him beamed with a ray of light as soon as her umbilical cord was cut.

Mornings came and mornings went with HS remaining in a relaxed state of mind. Ida, too, was happy, and she loved having HS happy and contented.

Finally, the day of departure! A neighbor and long-time friend came to take the family to the train depot. HS and his friend sat upfront on the wagon, saying nothing to each other as they rode down the quiet streets. HS glanced backwards only once, waving goodbye to the town of Winfield, Kansas as it rolled up behind him, closing the door to yet another chapter in his life.

1

*I*da's long slender fingers moved effortlessly over her tired worn face. Hypnotized by the rhythmic motions of the train, she neither felt nor heard anything. She did not hear the train whistle blow nor did she notice that the usually raucous Charles was quietly watching the passing countryside as though in a trance. Ida didn't react as Minnie shifted and snuggled against her father's strong, warm, and familiar body. Even the babbling sounds of the five-month old Bertha sitting on her lap did not rouse Ida, for she was far removed from her family's presence and the train's surroundings.

Thoughts of Winfield, Kansas raced through her mind faster than the trees passed before her eyes. Ida continued to stare out the window grappling with both the apprehension and the happiness of leaving Winfield.

There were many good days for the Pitts family in Winfield; however, there had also been many unsettling days. The growing season sometimes lasted for 200 days, many of which were spent in the wheat field from sun-up to sundown. Ida and HS had tilled the soil doggedly, competing with the best of farmers to make their yield enough to sustain the family. They worked hard because they knew how fortunate they were to be able to farm their own land. To be Black and able to work for oneself in Kansas was a measurable feat of which she remained forever grateful; however, 'making ends meet' was a real challenge! As Ida rode the train toward Montrose, Colorado, HS's beautiful bride counted her blessings.

Pauline S. Hill

As the train chugged down the tracks, Ida dreamed of days ahead. She had heard so much about the courageous Sojourner Truth, Harriet Tubman, and Frederick Douglass, until she began to conjure up the image of one of her children being as brave, prolific and renowned. Would one of her children make a difference in the lives of her people, a difference in the world? How foolish to have such dreams, she thought. Yet, as foolish as the dreams might have seemed, she could not dismiss them.

Ida was forced back to reality by Charles, who was still being quite a 'young man' but who would reach over to be sure that his baby sister was really there. Charles made a point not to ignore Minnie; he would tug at one of her braids or pinch her nose. He would then return to watch the world outside that kept passing by.

Ida looked down at Charles and wondered would her first-born be the one? What about Minnie her second born? Would her baby-girl, Bertha, be the one? Which of her children would add his or her name to the historical roster?

Charles, Minnie, and baby girl, Bertha, had done their portion of helping HS and Ida through the train ride. However, the long trip itself with the many stops in small towns and the slow, bumpy, winding pace had worn out the family's physical and mental strength. They were more than delighted when the conductor bellowed out, "Next stop, Montrose, Colorado!"

2

*I*n Montrose, the streets near the depot were lined with people waving in frantic anticipation. Montrose had grown since its founding in 1882. Being a service center for the miners and railroad workers, the town boasted a population of approximately 1,000 residents. On a brisk day in November of 1889, nearly all of them welcomed the train.

Some had stood for hours in the inclement weather to meet friends and relatives; some were there as they were each day – just to see the gigantic, screaming locomotive as it screeched into town. Others were there because the train reminded them of prosperity. After all, the mines and the railroads had made Colorado very rich and famous. Everyone seemed to be mesmerized by the train, everyone except Eliza Butler.

The short, slim ex-slave, whose manner and posture were as genteel, yet as powerful as the orations of Frederick Douglass or Sojourner Truth, leaned against one of the town's wooden framed structures. Her very demeanor reminded an onlooker of Colorado at its best. With an air of royalty second only to African queens, Eliza gazed at the train, holding on to her inner joy, enthusiasm, and optimism, for it had been years since she had seen her Ida! "My baby," thought Ida, had grown up to be quite a lady. She had a wonderful husband and three children of her own. Eliza wondered whether Ida had changed! Was she still the adorable, quick-witted person she had always known? Had the years kept her beautiful and slim or had three babies added extra pounds and wrinkles to her? Just what were Ida's children like, wondered Eliza.

Eliza shifted to her left foot and mentally chastised herself. She should be grateful and happy with whatever stepped from the train, she thought. She smiled smugly, however, when she thought of the neighbor reading her the letter that told about the new granddaughter that Ida and HS named Bertha. This pleased Eliza to no end even though she did not immediately know why except that she thought the grandchild named Bertha might be the one to do the reading and writing she could never do. Perhaps, she thought, Bertha might even be the one to learn about the vast "U - S of A" that Eliza had always wanted to explore. For a few moments, Eliza found contentment in her fantasy.

Eliza felt the cold wind whisk through her body, yet her hands were all warm and clammy. She did not want to feel this way. Eliza wanted to be calm and serene as she stared at the passengers climbing down from the train. She spotted Ida carrying what must be her new granddaughter. She gasped, a choking sound emanating from her mouth as she pushed her way through the crowd, calling out her daughter's name.

Ida heard her name and recognized her mother's clear tenor tone. In what seemed like one motion, she handed little Bertha to HS and thrust her handbag into Charles' hand.

"Mama, Mama, Mama!"

Charles gazed at Ida in disbelief. "Could my mama really have a mama of her very own?" he thought.

Charles stared at Ida and Eliza as the two clung to each other. Both were sobbing, hugging, and laughing simultaneously. Charles knew from his mother's eyes that she was quite happy.

HS handed little Bertha to his mother-in-law and the stately Eliza wept openly. Holding onto little Bertha, she reached out to Minnie and Charles, and the family climbed aboard the buggy and headed towards Eliza's home, the place where the family would live. In the buggy, HS made room for Minnie; little Bertha snuggled against Eliza, and Charles, looking quite like the first-born, smiled pleasantly thinking, "Montrose, Colorado at last!"

*D*ays turned into weeks and weeks into months. The Pitts family was finally able to move into their own home. Charles, wanting to help the family, convinced his daddy that he was old enough to earn a pittance by running errands for the miners. HS agreed because it gave him an opportunity to spend more time with his son because there was so much to tell him. There were of course the 'birds and the bees' and the more serious discussion of who he was as a young Black boy growing up in America.

HS remembered many of the stories surrounding his birth in Monticello, Mississippi even though he could hardly remember how he knew them. He certainly could not remember his mother and father who, like Eliza, had lived in slavery. HS taught his son some of the German that he spoke so fluently, yet when Charles asked his daddy where he had learned it, HS was unable to tell him. HS, nonetheless, wanted his son to know as much about the Pitts lineage as HS himself knew. Traveling time to and from the mines was well spent.

In the meantime, settling into the new homestead was proving to be quite a struggle for Ida who seemed to be deluged with chores that appeared unending. Baby Bertha made a significant difference in Ida's life. She had become accustomed to not having diapers to change, having Minnie and Charles doing little things for themselves, as well as helping her out around the house. She had been able to get her household and her farming chores done quite successfully. The birth of Bertha changed all of that. Bertha demanded Ida's attention. The work was just too much for one person to do.

HS suggested to Ida that perhaps Eliza would be willing to help out. After all, the washing and ironing that Eliza did for income did not keep her busy for very long and Eliza always wanted to spend her extra time with Bertha anyway.

At first, Ida was reluctant for she had never depended on anyone before to help with the work, not even HS. How would it look if people were to think her incapable of being a mother to all of her children and a wife to HS? As she thought more about it, Ida realized that if her mother were to keep Bertha, there would be more time to devote to chores and the older children. She could certainly be the wife to HS that she had been when first they married. HS was working as many as twelve hours a day in the mines and Ida wanted him to be able to rest when he came home from work.

HS and Ida decided to let Bertha stay with her grandmother during the day, and soon after, Ida began to notice that Bertha and Eliza were becoming inseparable. Eliza showed her grandchild the nooks and crannies of Montrose and their relationship grew. A kind of silent consensus occurred among the adults. Bertha would live with her grandmother. It was settled.

The proud grandma delighted herself with fixing up Bertha's room. The impressionable little girl marveled at how her grandma could take the slightest thing and turn it into a thing of beauty. Bertha loved being at her grandma's because the elderly lady seemed so patient with her. She encouraged Bertha's curiosity and it seemed as if she never tired of the million questions that came her way.

From the very day Ida agreed to let Bertha live with Eliza, the loving grandmother lived her life believing that 'Bertha was the one!' Knowing that Montrose was an all-white town except for the Pitts and Butler families, Eliza Butler began immediately to 'size up' all of the kindergarten programs. Experience had taught her how to analyze the behavior of people; therefore, as she and Bertha made their almost daily trips through the town returning clothes here and there, Eliza observed and listened to everything and everyone around her. She maneuvered herself into the homes of the mistresses where kindergarten classes were being held long before Bertha was of kindergarten age. Eliza knew as far ahead as one year to which kindergarten Bertha would attend. She had done a pre-school selection so that Bertha could have the right start in life.

Bertha's life became synonymous with kindergarten. She was so involved and occupied in kindergarten that she hardly had time to marvel and get to know her two new brothers, Huey and Tom. As a matter of fact, she could hardly remember when they were born. She knew that thirteen or fourteen months separated the two, yet how could she have been so unaware of two births? It's not that she did not miss Ida, HS, Charles and Minnie, and it's not that she did not wonder about what they were doing, Eliza just kept her every waking moment occupied!

With learning being the primary focus of kindergarten, and with Bertha excelling in everything that was taught, there was no time to notice that she was the only Black person in the school. Her social adjustment, coupled with all the skills and concepts Bertha mastered, proved to Eliza that her pre-school inquiries were justified.

After seeing that her 'Little Miss' was adjusting so nicely to school, Eliza permitted Bertha to run down to the depot with the neighborhood children to watch the trains. Bertha had to assure her grandmother that she would come directly back home and not tarry too long. Bertha was beside herself in awe and wonderment when she realized that she now had the privilege of going to the depot with her friends.

*O*ne wintry evening after a busy day at kindergarten of reciting the ABC's and endless poems, the 'depot group' decided to race to their favorite spot. When it was time to leave the depot, something unusual happened: Bertha was not ready to leave. She was thinking about the times when she had walked to the depot with her grandmother. The two of them would take their time walking back home, with Eliza allowing Bertha to touch and explore. Eliza would answer all of Bertha's questions, especially about her brothers Huey and Tommy. Bertha's favorite story was the Pitts family's arrival from Winfield, Kansas.

Bertha assured her friends that she would not dawdle and be late. She took the route that she and her grandmother usually walked. With the cold caressing her little nose and the wind lapping at her exposed ears, she still felt warm and fuzzy inside as she thought about Eliza. She tugged at her homemade scarf and muff, remembering that not only did her grandmother make all her clothing, but that she also toiled at keeping them immaculate.

As she continued along the familiar path towards home, Bertha hummed some of the songs that Eliza would sing as she scrubbed on the rub-board, leaned over the old round black wash pot and pushed the clothes up and down with a stick, and hung the clothes out to dry on the makeshift clothes line. As Bertha continued to hum, she envisioned those black flat irons in the warm fireplace, and she thought that even though Eliza must have been exhausted on many days, she never showed Bertha any sign of being too tired for her.

Too Young to Be Old

The whistle from the mines snapped Bertha back to reality. She hastened her pace. She wanted to get home to the person whom she loved with all her heart, the person who would not have accepted any excuse for her getting home late.

When Bertha turned seven years old, the gay-spirited elderly Eliza convinced herself that her favorite grandchild was ready for the public school of Montrose. She had never been sick; she'd learned all of the basics and many first grade skills and concepts, and she had also become the best rock thrower in town. Eliza had seen Bertha and her friends take on some of the meanest rock throwers in town. Bertha was taken aback when her grandmother acknowledged knowing this. Yes, Bertha was definitely ready for public elementary school!

Bertha studied incessantly. Her adeptness allowed her to surpass most of her peers. She could memorize the longest passages and decipher, interpret, or decode better than most of the second and third graders. Furthermore, she had mastered at least three foreign languages, translating them fluently. She won nearly all of the spelling bees. This enthusiasm for learning prevailed throughout her elementary school days. Eliza believed that an education was the key to everything so she encouraged Bertha to learn, for she realized that being Black meant Bertha had to be better than her White counterparts. Eliza never spoke these words to Bertha; however, everything that Eliza did was strategically planned in order for Bertha to excel because Eliza knew and understood what was going on in the world.

Four things were equal to Bertha's search for knowledge: she still liked to visit the depot; she enjoyed doing things with her grandmother; she loved coasting down the banks of Montrose in the winter; and 'hayrack' riding in the summer. "The moonlit hayrack rides with Grandma Butler and our other friends were always the best."

During Bertha's elementary days, Eliza always exemplified wisdom. She recognized that both an education and playtime were necessary but that they alone did not make an individual well-rounded. Her 'Little Miss' would also be taught how to work. Bertha was made to help with the chores of the day.

"When Grandma Butler was doing the wash for a local resident or eating establishment, not only did I have to press the front of the garment, but I had to smooth the opposite side and press the front again – all with those flatirons. I became very adept with the flatiron cleaning and heating routine.

"I was taught to mend and scrub. I learned to clean the lamp chimneys, to make soap and to make straw brooms and mattresses."

Furthermore, Eliza saw to it that Bertha's life was filled with religious zeal. Bertha was required to participate in all of the youth programs that were a part of the Montrose Congregational Church, which in 1981 became known as the United Church of Christ.

*T*eachers at Montrose High School had already received the news about Bertha's intelligence long before she enrolled there in 1903. She excelled in high school even more than she had in elementary school. She especially liked German, for whenever she did get a chance to visit her family, she could converse with her daddy in German. This proved to be invaluable practice for her, and moreover, it took HS' mind off her inability to cook. Minnie always captured the cooking honors and Bertha detested having the subject come up at family gatherings.

Bertha studied for long hours so that she could please the adults in her life. She worked so hard that she hardly noticed when her brother Charles left home. Charles was now 'keeping house' on his own. This saddened her momentarily for she realized that she hardly knew Charles at all. In fact, she hadn't spent much time with Huey and Tom or for that matter with her sister Minnie either. She wouldn't get that chance now because Minnie had, relatively early, married one of the miners and had begun a family of her own in Montana. Did Huey and Tom know anything about her, Bertha wondered?

Each day when the teachers asked how many hours were spent studying a particular subject, Bertha felt proud when it was she who could report the most. It was always deemed important to study for a long time.

Surprisingly, Bertha's peers seemed extremely pleased about her ability to learn. An outsider might have thought that being the only Black student in her class and maintaining top honors in nearly all of her subjects would have caused internal unrest among the White students and adults, but to the contrary, everyone encouraged her. The Pitts and Butler families, the only two Black families in the town, were highly regarded and respected in Montrose.

In 1908, the town heard the valedictory address recited eloquently by Bertha Pitts who had finished her high school years *summa cum laude*, which denoted the highest academic standing in her class. Bertha Pitts had maintained the highest scholastic average in her class and she was highlighted, spotlighted, and celebrated.

Eliza, HS, Ida, Huey, Tom and Charles joined the family to celebrate. They were all 'besides themselves,' with joy and jubilation. Their radiance reverberated throughout the entire community when they learned that Bertha had won a four-year scholarship to Colorado College in Colorado Springs, Colorado. Eliza thanked the good Lord; her strategy, planning, and sacrificing had paid off.

The family rejoiced as they all settled together for the first time in a long time to count their blessings. They wished with all their hearts that Minnie could be with them, but Dillon, Montana was just too far away. Minnie and her family sent their regrets and their fondest regards.

3

As the family busied themselves with planning Bertha's departure for Colorado Springs, a member of Bertha's church was also making plans which would alter the course of Bertha's life.

Montrose was by no means isolated from the rest of the world. People there knew that the Civil War had not really ended slavery, and that many Blacks were worse off economically than they had been prior to the beginning of the war. Freed men and women (those who separated themselves from the plantation) were in dire need of all kinds of help. The Reconstruction Period had ended and the political, economic, and educational gains of Blacks were deteriorating. A few Blacks were achieving, some had even attained educational degrees, but this was only a 'drop in the bucket!' In order to alleviate some of the suffering, concerned Americans urged Congress to form the Freedmen's Bureau. It was created on March 3, 1865.

The Bureau acted as an extension of the War Department and gave protection, organization, and financial aid to freed men and the states. After the war, the Bureau helped to establish elementary and secondary schools as well as institutions of higher learning for Black Americans.

General Oliver Otis Howard was a United States General, a staunch Congregationalist and a leading founder of the Freedmen's Bureau. One of the institutions of higher learning founded by the Bureau was Howard University in Washington,

D.C., so named to honor the valor of General Howard. Oliver Otis Howard became the first president of Howard University in 1869 and served until 1873.

So, a progressive thinking church member of Bertha's Congregationalist Church wanted to send an astute Black student to the school that was founded by and named for one of the highest ranking persons in the Congregationalist Church. The member told Bertha and her family first about General Howard and the Freedmen's Bureau. In this conversation, highlights of other prominent Blacks were shared, most notably Phyllis Wheatley, Harriet Tubman, Mary Eliza Church Terrell, W.E.B. Dubois, and Frederick Douglass. Finally came the information about Howard University, the institution for Negroes that was founded by the General and supported by the Congregationalist Church.

Bertha stored the information carefully away in her mind and as carefully, watched the expression on the faces of her parents and grandmother, for she had always wanted to know more about her people. The little she'd heard and knew about Black people just wasn't enough!

The church member explained to the family that the Bureau had set aside monies for the personal needs of individuals and that the home church would bear any expenses that the Bureau did not cover.

Eliza, HS, and Ida talked about what it would be like for Bertha to experience an all-Black environment since she had only been in a predominately all-White one all her life. The more they talked, the more they knew that this would be a glorious experience for Bertha. Eliza realized that Bertha would see the vast United States that they all always wanted to see. Yet, Washington, D.C. was such a long way from Montrose, Colorado, she thought.

A few days later, Eliza gave her approval, as did HS and Ida. Bertha rejoiced in the chance to finally experience her people *en masse* and she was simply overjoyed!

This time, Bertha, an adult, found herself enroute to her childhood haven, the town's depot. Rather than just meeting the train to revel in its beauty and strength, she would board it for Washington, D.C.

"An education is the gateway to everything!" Eliza Butler repeated to herself over and over again as she and Bertha took their familiar route to the depot. Ida and HS understood the personal connection between the two; therefore, they went ahead of them, carrying the huge trunk which took up most of the space on the back of the wagon.

Most of Bertha and Eliza's walking time was spent in silence for while they were happy, they were both sad and not quite sure which emotion was the stronger. They often stared and smiled at each other. At one point they walked with their arms around each other. They arrived at the depot and approached not only HS and Ida, but half of the church people as well! As Bertha beamed with pride and thanksgiving, she was glad that she and her grandmother had walked alone for now it was apparent that she would have to greet and be cordial to nearly half of Montrose.

Bertha was her usually polite self, showing gratitude to all. As her eyes wandered over the huge crowd, stopping to gaze into the faces of well-wishers most of whom she knew quite well, she suddenly missed not having Minnie there. Again she thought about how long it had been since she last saw her sister and now it would be much, much longer. She thought about how she could write to her and capture in a letter all those things they had missed about each other while growing up.

Bertha heard the words, "All aboard!" and momentarily lost her breath. How many times had she stood there looking up and admiring that huge train, hearing the conductor say those very words, while wishing she could climb aboard. Now, in a few seconds, she was going to do just that! She would climb aboard!

HS, her handsome hardworking father, holding back tears muttered in German, "Ich Liebe Dich" and she responded as she hugged him tightly, "Ich Liebe Dich" (I love you)! Bertha hugged Ida warmly and reminded her to bid adieu to her brothers Charles, Huey, and Tom.

Finally, Bertha walked over to her grandmother and all of her sadness, happiness, and joy were wrapped into the special hug that was mixed with warm tears streaming down both their faces. Between what had now become sobs from them both, Eliza was asking fifty questions about did she bring this or that!

"All aboard!"

Bertha made her way to the train, climbed aboard, found her seat hurriedly and began waving even before the train pulled away. She waved and waved and waved even after she could no longer recognize her family and the townspeople who'd come to see her go where most of them had only heard, read or dreamed about.

*B*ertha settled in on the train and kept her purse close to her side. She took out her little change purse periodically to savor the sight of the $5 gold piece given to her by a well-wisher at the depot. Bertha also checked her wallet for the money she herself had acquired for the trip. This money was special because her grandmother helped her to earn it, and because it would allow Bertha to fulfill a life-long fantasy! "I saved up and saved up so that I could eat one meal in that dining car. I knew that one day, I'd ride that train and eat in that dining car!"

So many delightful and fanciful stories about the elegance of the dining car and the delicious-tasting food which was served had been shared with her by travelers ever since she was a little girl. Each time she caught a glimpse of the dining car, she could hardly catch her breath.

Now, at last! At long last, Bertha Adine Pitts was aboard the train and was ready to pay for her own meal that she would eat in the exquisite dining car! She exhaled! She really had problems controlling her breathing! The finger bowls glistened at her; the water in them was clear enough to drink! The chandeliers sparkled brighter than any she'd seen in Montrose! It seemed like the one above her table could brighten the entire town of Montrose! The table cloth shone brighter than the white coat that her waiter wore; not even a doctor's coat shone so brightly!

Knowing who the young lady was and where she was going spotlighted Bertha from the moment she stepped foot onto the train. The dining car waiter especially wanted to please her. He brought her a meal more scrumptious and decoratively placed than the elegance of the dining car! "The service would befit a queen," she thought!

Bertha ate the food allowing the taste to linger after each bite. A couple sitting at the adjoining table asked her a question and she answered politely but quickly so that she could give the car and her food the attention they deserved! She wished with all of her might that her grandmother could have shared these joys with her. She knew though, that Eliza would have wanted her to do just what she was doing: enjoying that moment and each moment of her train ride.

The stopover in Chicago was fascinating! Chicago was different than Montrose. Everyone seemed in a hurry! Also, there was more construction going on in Chicago than there ever was in Montrose. She wished that she could have ventured farther than four streets away from the depot to see more, but she dared not. While walking back to the train, she turned into a little 'all purpose' store to buy some postal cards. She hurried back to the train and wrote a few lines to Eliza.

Having written the card, she checked with the conductor to see whether she had enough time to mail it. He assured her by telling her that the train would be in Chicago for another hour or so. Bertha looked around for a post office. A Chicagoan pointed out that Chicago had few post offices but many mailboxes. He described a mailbox to her and pointed her down the street.

"I went to this box and attempted to deposit my card only to discover that I was trying to mail my card in a fire alarm box. Chicago was *quite* different than Montrose."

After three days of jostling about on the train, taking in the wide terrain and small towns, and talking to many people from different places, Bertha arrived in Washington, D.C. extremely exhausted but equally excited!

4

The trip from the depot to Howard University was an experience in itself! The greatest sights were the White House and the Washington Monument. "Why," thought Bertha, "they look just like the pictures in the history books." She stared and stared at all the beautiful Black people she encountered. They were black, brown, yellow, and tan – all colors of beautiful Black people. She wanted to act natural; she tried very hard, however, no one was there to tell her how she was doing!

Minor Hall Girls Dormitory at Howard University Teachers College became Bertha's new home. As she approached her living quarters, she made one profound observation: Howard had very 'modern' facilities - gas and electrical lights! Bertha smiled, knowing that she did not have to clean the kerosene lamp chimneys anymore.

At Howard, the students had to take care of themselves. Bertha was grateful that her grandmother had taught her how to wash, iron, and care for her personal needs. Knowing how to do the various chores proved to be most essential. "I could not understand when some of the girls could not properly take care of themselves. Many of them had to get others to do things for them. Perhaps some of their dependence was due to their middle class affluence. Many of the students were well to do; you could tell by the quality of their clothing."

The young ladies worked well together in order to adjust to their new surroundings. There were no social class distinctions. They gladly supported each other because from the day they walked onto the Howard campus until they became sophomores, they were made to bear the brunt of all the upperclassmen's jokes and antics.

All the students, though, worked together to prepare themselves for the upcoming curriculums. Bertha, after scrutinizing her schedule, felt that her stringent high school curriculums had prepared her well for what was to come. She could tell that Howard was serious business. The professors and the staff at Howard were dedicated, intelligent, and very, very strict. The upperclassmen while continuing their antics against the freshmen, helped tremendously by advising the freshmen about the different personalities and expectations of the professors.

Dean Moore had a way with words that could cut a person down quicker than HS' scythe could cut a stalk, Bertha learned. His favorite saying was, "It's better to have a fifty cents hat on a one dollar head, than to have a one dollar hat on a fifty cents head." So the freshmen were told to always be alert and submit all assignments in Dean Moore's class.

Alain Leroy Locke (1886-1954), critic and chronicler of the Harlem Renaissance and first Black Rhodes Scholar, came to Howard from Oxford University. Alain Locke became Bertha's philosophy professor. "I have not understood what Alain Leroy Locke was talking about to this day. He was 'too deep' for me, but I completed all of his work."

Ernest Edward Just (1883-1941), the renowned biologist was Bertha's physiology professor; Benjamin Brawley (1882 – 1939), a South Carolinian who was a noted historian, became Bertha's English professor. The famous mathematician and sociologist, Kelly Miller (1863 – 1939) always emphasized to his students, Eliza Butler's philosophy of 'an education being the gateway to everything!' Bertha loved his classes.

The upperclassmen convinced the newcomers that they wanted more physical education classes. The professors, however, were adamant about scheduling only enough P.E. to stimulate the body and the mind. Not even a minute was allowed for wasting time. The upperclassmen expressed hope that perhaps they, along with the freshmen, could band together to request that there be more physical education classes because P.E. should not be considered as a waste of time.

After some days of settling in and becoming acquainted with college life and her new surroundings, Bertha began to write letters. She could only write one letter per night, but she was determined that her grandmother, HS, Ida, Minnie, members of her church back home, and all her friends would hear about her experiences from her first. She closed each letter with the joking revelation of how she lost that $5 gold piece that she'd tried so earnestly to protect.

5

*B*ertha had an exceptional first year academically at Howard; she was as avid a learner in college as she had been in high school. Literature remained one of Bertha's favorite classes for she loved the works of Paul Laurence Dunbar, John Milton, Henry Wadsworth Longfellow, Edgar Allan Poe, and others. "They also serve who stand and wait;" and "The Day is Done," were among Bertha's favorite quoted works. She would always say that, "People need a verse or a quote because when a person gets into trouble with others or himself or herself, what will they do if they cannot find one verse to recite for consolation or for help?"

Social life for Bertha was marred however by the prejudicial and racial attitudes that prevailed in Washington, D.C. and surrounding towns. Oh, D.C. was beautiful enough around the nation's capital area, but Bertha felt racial hatred, something she had never known before. She was completely sheltered from bigotry in Montrose. Washington, D.C. was a lesson to be learned! Bertha's only recourse was to rely on her past experiences of respect, tolerance, and perseverance, learn as much as she could from her peers, and balance her experiences and acquired knowledge with the present-day realization that attitudes and actions were changing *slowly* in the south, if at all.

The students seldom, if ever, ventured away from the campus because they could literally starve to death downtown before any of the establishments would serve them. Shopping was no fun either because, if they had extra money, they knew better than to try on a garment before purchasing it. The practice of trying on garments was unheard of for Blacks in Washington, D.C.! "Jim Crow" was all around her: "Jim Crow stores!" "Jim Crow water!" "Jim Crow toilets!" Bertha was especially taken aback by the "Jim Crow train!"

All of her life Bertha had grown up idolizing and admiring the huge iron machine. The last time she made a local trip, she was escorting two small White children to and from Washington, D.C. to Virginia as a part-time babysitter. Bertha noticed that her people were being escorted to a special car in the rear of the train. She wanted so badly to go back there to ask them how they felt about how they were being treated. She wasn't, however, allowed to leave the children.

Bertha could not bear the humiliation. She kept the part-time job of babysitter for several months after that but she did not ever agree to escort the children on the train again.

Writing letters home became a frequent pastime now for Bertha because she could unburden her emotions on paper and contemplate what her grandmother would say in reply if she were near or if she could write a letter of her own. Bertha could not believe that the attitudes of the whites in Colorado were so drastically different from the attitudes of the whites in Washington, D.C. And yet, in fact, they were very different!

*H*er freshman year was over; a whole year had passed, and Bertha remained in Washington, D.C. her first summer. Summer school had been an option and she took advantage of that opportunity. Little did she know how much she would regret that decision.

Pauline S. Hill

That summer of 1909, the love of her life left this world. She did not get a chance to say goodbye to her grandmother; she would not have a chance to see her again; she would never have the opportunity to walk to the depot again with Eliza. Eliza would never hear all the stories about the United States and her first year at Howard that Bertha was unable to share in her letters. Bertha had dreamed many days of all the things she would share with her grandmother whenever they were together again. Now, that time would never come. One could never begin to know the incredible agony Bertha felt when she received that telegram informing her about Eliza's death. She found herself humming some of Eliza's favorite songs and after she cried what seemed like hours, she found comfort in verses that she remembered – "She walks in beauty like the night ..." "Oh my love is like a red, red rose ...." She recited many poems aloud and silently, and she sang and hummed more songs in order to gain the solace she needed to ease the pain of losing her dear grandmother, and the strength to go on.

Obtaining a good education became an obsession after Eliza's death. Bertha studied more zealously than before; all she could think about was rewarding her grandmother, posthumously.

During the latter part of Bertha's sophomore year, she began to sense a kind of unrest in the air. Students were buzzing about the Niagara Movement and how the strength of that predominately Black political organization had morphed into the founding of the National Association for the Advancement of Colored People (NAACP), in 1909, by Black leaders like Ida B. Wells and W.E.B. Dubois along with several White leaders. The talk of a women's movement that targeted women's rights to vote began to permeate the campus. Bertha noticed that her own attitude of tolerance was slowly diminishing. Groups that had formed originally for purposes of social cohesiveness now became vehicles for rising feelings of social unrest. The unrest did not affect Bertha's life directly until 1913, her senior year.

Bertha and several other young ladies joined a Greek letter sorority, Alpha Kappa Alpha Sorority, the first Black Greek letter sorority (1908) in the United States. The new members were hoping that the sorority would undertake the task of designing innovative approaches to address the injustices and inequalities that were paramount in the area. The sorority had been doing this indirectly but because this was not the major thrust of this group of young women, the newcomers introduced a new agenda, which was not accepted! The old members were adamantly opposed to a thrust that was more 'politically than socially driven.' Dissatisfaction abound!

Because the new members were not able to get their new agenda adopted as part of the sorority's major thrust, they realized that they could not be contented with being members of a social organization when there existed around them so much bigotry, turmoil, and racial prejudices. The newcomers were inspired by the Black forerunners and present day activists like Mary Eliza Church Terrell and Ida B. Wells who were organizing groups of African American women and men to work to end oppression. They were equally inspired by the suffragettes (women who worked to obtain the right to vote for all women) who had been in Washington, D.C. for some time recruiting supporters and marchers to advocate for the rights of women to vote.

It was at this point that Delta was born. Twenty-two women accepted the call to form their own sisterhood.

After brainstorming purposes and goals, the twenty-two requested assistance from E.P. Davis, their Greek professor, regarding the selection of a suitable name for the group. He questioned the young ladies about their disenfranchising themselves from Alpha Kappa Alpha Sorority. He knew what the Sorority meant to the other members, to the staff, and students at Howard. He had to be certain that there would be no lingering animosity because he did not want any dissension or any unrest that might divide the campus.

After understanding and trusting the purpose of the group of young women who had come before him, Professor Davis suggested to the ladies that the name Delta Sigma Theta seemed to be an excellent choice for the forming organization. The professor further explained that among the many meaning, *Delta* meant fourth in order of brightness; it was the fourth letter of the Greek alphabet and would be the fourth Black Greek letter fraternal organization; and, *Sigma* meant *the sum of.* There was no rationale given for Theta that Bertha could remember.

The ladies expressed their gratitude to Professor Davis and agreed to go forth to establish their own sorority. Hence, at Howard University on January 13, 1913, Bertha Pitts became one of the twenty-two founding members of Delta Sigma Theta Sorority, Alpha Chapter. The purpose of Delta Sigma Theta Sorority stated in the incorporation papers read: To establish and maintain a high standard of morality and scholarship among women of the School of Liberal Arts at Howard University.

Bertha and her sisters elected Myra Davis (Hemmings) as the first president of Alpha Chapter. Myra Davis and the chapter members busied themselves writing rules and procedures; they contacted other campuses to establish chapters. The Deltas wanted to extend their sisterhood because they knew that there was power in numbers!

Myra Davis was deemed a good president and served until graduation in May at which time Madree Penn (White) became the second president. Madree Penn succeeded in establishing Beta Chapter at Wilberforce University in Ohio in 1914.

Deltas were alive to everything occurring about them. They watched the plans and learned from the strategies of the suffragettes. Early in March of 1913, Washington, D.C. was erupting in excitement! Woodrow Wilson had been elected as the 28th President of the United States and a great inaugural parade was scheduled for March 4th. In a strategic move, after several state conventions and many meetings, the suffragettes secured the third of March for a 'right to vote' parade.

The newly formed Delta Chapter was ecstatic about the news. Deltas knew that they had to work as hard as The NAACP, Ida Wells, Mary Church Terrell, W.E. B. Dubois, Mary McLeod Bethune and all those who were working to secure justice and equality for Black Americans. They studied and watched very carefully the foci and outcomes of the female leadership that was setting a precedent for women and other suppressed and oppressed people in this country. Thus, the win of the suffragettes for the right to vote parade felt like a Delta victory and they rejoiced.

Ida B. Wells, a journalist, who'd been working for justice since the late 19th century, organized the Alpha Suffrage Club among Black women in Chicago and they were planning to march in the parade. Mary Church Terrell, meanwhile, was also organizing Black women to march in the right to vote parade.

Bertha and her sisters were amazed when Myra Davis, their president, secured permission for the members of the sorority to participate in the march. "How she did this was amazing to us all because the permission had to come from both the president of the university and the chairman of the parade committee." This was no easy feat because there had been much debate over whether to let Black women participate in the march at all. In the south, there was much opposition to women suffrage because legislators feared that if women were given the vote, the vote might be given to Black people which would outnumber the votes of Whites. This drove fear throughout the country and especially the south. What then could be a compromise, especially after the scathing editorial in the _Crisis Magazine_ by W.E.B. Dubois in June 1912. In what was thought of as a compromise, a decision was made to let Black women march in the back of the parade which did not set well with the women, especially Ida B. Wells.

Pauline S. Hill

When the Deltas received the news that they would be allowed to march with the suffragettes, they were delighted. In fact, they were as pleased to escape from the campus as they were serious about the march!

Bertha and the other Deltas who were seniors wore their caps and gowns in the parade. As they marched down the streets of D.C. from the U.S. Capitol past the White House among more than 8,000 women, Bertha noticed the reactions of the onlookers. "Some cheered, however, many jeered and tried to disrupt the marchers by throwing things, spitting on, beating, and slapping the women, and trying to pull the women off the floats. The police gave little protection to the women, thereby showing sympathy for the opposition to women's suffrage."

Bertha, Myra, Madree, and the other Delta sorors finished the parade and for the first time since her arrival in Washington, D.C., Bertha felt as if she had made a statement to the nation's capital and to the nation itself!

Bertha graduated *cum laude* (with academic honors and praise) from Howard University Teachers College in June of 1913 and received a Bachelor of Arts degree in Education.

6

In the mid 1800's, many Blacks under the leadership of escaped slave, Benjamin "Pap" Singleton (1809 – 1892) who was known as the "Father of the Negro Exodus," had migrated to the Kansas area. In the early 1900's, community leaders were aiding Blacks in setting up schools to educate illiterate young African Americans in the area. Howard University's placement office convinced Bertha that Topeka, Kansas needed her and many other trained students whom they felt would make good teachers.

The teaching assignment was ideal to Bertha because she was not ready to go home to face Montrose without her grandmother, nor was she prepared to begin a career at home where she might have been scrutinized by family and/or friends. Therefore, Bertha accepted the teaching position at Topeka Industrial Educational Institute.

Older, wiser and worldlier, Bertha left Howard University with her degree tucked carefully away. Her four years at Howard had been interesting years for her. As she thought of the omnipresent changing social trends in the world, she also reminisced about the good old days. What would Eliza say if she could see her now, she thought! Further, she pondered and wondered about her upcoming teaching assignment! Could she become as effective in teaching as Professors Brawley, Locke, or any of her Howard University professors? Would the push for freedom for Blacks and women, the Industrial Revolution, the ever-popular new and changing music, or any of the rapidly changing social trends have an impact on her and her pupils? Would the people in Kansas be more like the people in Montrose or those in Washington, D.C.? All these questions led Bertha to a state of anxiety!

In the little rural school of Topeka, Bertha taught everything. She found it difficult to adjust to the grouping she had to do in spelling, reading, mathematics, and history. No two pupils seemed at the same academic readiness. Bertha discovered that many of her students were much bigger and in many instances, much older than she. Furthermore, her lifelong eagerness for knowledge would not let her accept her pupils' lack of interest in learning.

Nineteen fourteen moved along and Bertha could no longer hide her displeasure with being a teacher. She tried hard to be fair in her assessment of the situation. Perhaps it wasn't all the fault of her pupils; she knew that she was not the same person after Eliza's death and marching with the suffragettes had profoundly altered her outlook, ideals, and her life. Whatever the reason, Bertha realized that teaching was not for her. She had to get away from Topeka Industrial Educational Institute as quickly as possible.

Bertha contacted Howard Teachers College and inquired about employment there. She secured a job! Hurriedly submitting a letter of resignation effective the end of her one year as teacher, she found herself aboard another train headed for Washington, D.C.

Washington, D.C. bustled. President Woodrow Wilson was busily establishing commissions and passing acts. Construction had begun on the Lincoln Memorial; people were questioning the gains of the suffragettes, as well as the gains – or lack thereof – for Black people. Many whispered about the war. Bertha could still sense however, that Washington, D.C. had not essentially changed as far as African Americans and women were concerned. There still was that aura of keeping Blacks and women in their places.

Bertha felt relief in believing that this year was going to be a good one for her. Her feelings were totally confirmed when Marie Hardwick, the preceptress, which is now called the 'Dean of Women,' welcomed her back to Minor Hall. Receiving her new appointment as assistant preceptress with humility, Bertha expressed gratitude for the job and vowed to give it her full attention. She lost herself in her work and enjoyed helping the young people in Minor Hall and in the Sorority. For almost two years, Bertha served as assistant preceptress in Minor Hall.

Howard University became a mental refuge for Bertha. She renewed her kinships and acquaintances; she became involved with fighting injustices; she joined her sorors and found them warm, congenial, and incessantly working towards their goals.

The Sorority was organizing chapters and collecting strength across the country: establishing chapters at the University of Pennsylvania, the University of Iowa, and the University of Ohio. The Sorority was also inviting prominent and influential women to honorary membership. Contacted and invited were women like Mary Church Terrell, (1863 – 1954), educator, lecturer, speaker, writer, fighter for equal rights, and author of the Delta Creed, and Mary McLeod Bethune (1875 – 1955), founder and president of the Daytona Normal and Industrial Institute for Negro Girls (now, Bethune-Cookman College). Other women, along with Nannie Helen Burroughs (1879 – 1961) founder and president of the National Training School for Women and Girls who was influential in the struggle for the rights of women, were also invited to join the organization. Delta women were on the move.

At what was almost the pinnacle of success for her, sad, sad news once again reached the energetic, young Bertha. Another telegram: Minnie had died in Dillon, Montana! Oh how Bertha lamented! How could her *only* sister be dead? Bertha had just heard from her about one month earlier and nothing, absolutely nothing was mentioned about Minnie being ill! Bertha was planning to spend the upcoming summer with Minnie! She had worked out all of the details in her head, including saving for the trip because it had been so long since she'd seen her sister. She knew very little about her brother-in-law and his family and she wanted so much to meet her two nieces and nephew whom she had never seen. The oldest must have been nearly thirteen now. From the letters that she and Minnie had exchanged, she had formed images in her head; however, images were one thing, Bertha thought, but seeing and touching were entirely different. Bertha agonized over not knowing her sister and her sister's family better; now it was too late, and it seemed ironic to Bertha that in life she had very little time for her *only* sister. Now that death had claimed Minnie, she would now be able to fully focus on her sister, a feat she was unable to accomplish during Minnie's lifetime. She prayed for life after death!

*D*illon, Montana!

So that's where Minnie had lived ...and died! Dillon, situated in a wide agricultural valley with the Continental Divide running straight through the county and wrapping around it. Dillon, which in 1805 had witnessed its first White men brought to the area by Meriwether Lewis and Captain William Clark. Dillon, where just west in Bannack, the cry of gold in 1862 was heard. Dillon, finally connected by railroad, and named for Sydney Dillon, the Union Pacific Railroad president, and which in 1881 received the county seat that was originally in Bannack. Dillon a rugged wilderness!

Did any of this matter to Minnie and her family? It did not matter much to Bertha at the time for she hardly saw the place; she did not tarry at all. Packing her nieces and nephew as fast as she could, she set out for Grand Junction, Colorado. Minnie's in-laws lived in Grand Junction and even though Bertha did not know them, judging from Minnie's description of her husband's family in her letters, she knew that her nieces and nephew would be well cared for now that Minnie was gone! She prayed that Minnie would know this and rest in peace.

7

Grand Junction like the rest of the world was worried about the war. The United States was trying to persuade Germany and its allies to befriend Russia. President Woodrow Wilson worked very hard for world peace but to no avail. Everyone now was beginning to feel that active involvement in the war by the United States had become only a matter of time.

Everywhere Bertha turned, someone wanted to talk about the war. She was concerned about the affairs of the state; however, she was more concerned about her personal state of being. Life was moving too fast for her. No more Eliza, no more Minnie – both were gone. She had not heard from Huey, Tom, or Charles in years and she knew that death was just a matter of time for both HS and Ida. She found consolation in knowing that she could visit and love Minnie's children. She made a solemn vow to do so! Bertha was convinced that she had to establish some consistent direction to her life. Her life savings were dwindling and she had to make some decisions about where she would work and what she would do. At twenty-eight years of age, it seemed as if thinking and worrying had become too much of a way of life for her. She had not felt calm or relaxation in a very long time. She paced her steps to the depot.

At the depot, Bertha's measured steps led her to the ticket window where she fantasized about buying a ticket that would take her to beautiful, warm, sunny, and fun-loving California! As she looked around the dimly lit room, she couldn't help but notice this tall, suave, handsome, and debonair young man staring intently at her. At first she was hesitant to meet his eyes even though his gaze was quite captivating. Momentarily, she shyly glanced over at him and to her delight he was still staring at her and, oh no, he was beginning to saunter in her direction! Now, thought Bertha, what would Eliza have her do at a time like this?

Unbelievable! Simply, unbelievable! Could this be love at first sight? This short encounter began the next chapter in Bertha's life with Earl Allen Campbell.

The love of Bertha's life, the handsome Earl Allen Campbell

*E*arl Allen Campbell could not do enough for the tiny young lady whom he loved with all his heart. He courted her with a fervor that could have surpassed the greatest loves of all history! "How do I love thee, let me count the ways ...!" Not a trace remained of the sadness and concern that had pervaded her entire thinking days before.

When Earl Allen proposed, the smile on Bertha's face reverberated through her letter, and had he seen her beaming eyes, instead of reading her response, he would have seen how her eyes signaled her affirmative response. Bertha Pitts became Mrs. Earl Allen Campbell in 1917, just days before Russia withdrew from World War I and the United States declared war on Germany. "My ol' lady," as Earl Allen fondly called her, was happy, contented, and loved. She was as in love and she was loved and she was so very glad to have someone to take care of her.

Earl Allen continued to work as a custodian with the railroad in Grand Junction while Bertha busied herself becoming a competent wife and homemaker. A blissful year passed during which time Bertha became pregnant. The loving couple would always remember that their son was born the same year that World War I ended. Somehow in the Campbell's lives, their historical moments paralleled those of world affairs, so 1918 would be another year to remember forever.

Bertha adjusted to the conveniences of the day. She enjoyed her radio, electric lights and especially her sewing machine. Earl Allen helped her to renovate their little home and they kept it shining. When Earl was at work, Bertha would sit at her treadle sewing machine and sew for hours at a time. She enjoyed making coats, pants, and shirts for Earl Junior and sometimes even for Earl Allen.

Earl Allen Jr. 1920

Earl Allen enjoyed watching her with Earl Junior, always complimenting her on the way she kept him so neatly dressed with the garments she had made. He was glad that he'd bought her the sewing machine. It proved to be a very worthwhile gift.

Earl Junior was a pleasant and amusing child during the years that the Campbell family stayed in Grand Junction and in this period of time, Bertha suffered the loss of both her mother Ida and HS her beloved father. Earl Allen helped her through these sorrowful times as only he could. Bertha was very grateful that he was with her because he helped to make a way for her when there seemed to have been no way out of her state of being. Earl Junior and Minnie's children also added comfort and joy to her spirit. She did not want to focus on the fact that her losses were 'adding up.'

When Earl Junior was five years old, Earl Allen broke the news to Bertha that his brother, Henry Campbell, who lived in Seattle, Washington, wanted them to move to the Pacific Northwest. Henry explained to Earl that Seattle was a progressive city with weather that was quite Mediterranean and that he really wanted his brother and his family nearby.

Bertha remembered what it had meant to her to grow up with her grandmother and she figured that if Earl Junior could experience a similar warm closeness with his relatives, then, why not move to Seattle? Besides, she told herself that Seattle was close to California, and perhaps she would at last have the opportunity to see the place that she had dreamed about for so long.

Bertha and Earl Allen busied themselves sorting their accumulated possessions. They made last visits to friends and finally went over to see Minnie's children. With tears in her eyes and heaviness in her heart, Bertha embraced her nieces and her nephew and bade them goodbye. She promised to always remember them and to keep in touch.

8

In 1923, the Campbell family boarded the old iron horse and began their journey to Seattle, Washington. Bertha's thoughts of the new frontier were all positive and optimistic. Best of all was the anticipation of that beautiful California-like weather. When they arrived on July 4, 1923, it was raining!

As the Campbell's began their new life in the Pacific Northwest, several things became very apparent. The fantastic scenery was breathtakingly beautiful. The beautiful California-like sunshine, however, remained in California. Most of the time, it was cold and rainy, and cold and rainy remained an omnipresent reality! If she could have had her way, Bertha and her family would have returned to Colorado. Seattle was now their home she thought and because their supply of money was running low, they would have to make the best of their situation. They roomed in private homes to economize and Earl Allen took on odd jobs at various places to make ends meet.

Soon thereafter and very fortunately so, Earl Allen became employed by the United State Immigration and Naturalization Service. He enjoyed his work as a custodian, elevator operator, and security guard. After several months in Seattle, the Campbell family realized to their surprise and delight that they were really very happy. They loved Seattle, each other, and Earl Junior as much as they relished their new quality of life.

They bought and moved into their own house, and Bertha's days settled into a very contented routine. She joined Seattle's

First African Methodist Episcopal Church (First A.M.E.), and since church had always been a part of her existence, she saw to it that Earl Junior also learned the principles of the church.

Bertha loved the worship service at First A.M.E. and she reveled in learning the history of the A.M.E. Church. Before delving into the history of her local church in Seattle, she became fascinated with the origin of the African Methodist Church which was started in 1787 by a 27-year-old Black leader, Richard Allen. She learned that Black people, many of whom were ex-slaves, were expected to worship quietly in St. George Methodist Episcopal Church, the White church, in Philadelphia. Blacks were treated inhumanely in their worship experience at St. George, therefore, in 1787, Richard Allen politely walked out of St. George Church and began a movement that recognized as its spiritual doctrine: "God as our Father, Christ as our Redeemer, and Man as our Brother." Bertha appreciated that Richard Allen knew how important it was for people of African descent to be able to worship freely and to be treated with respect and dignity. For a brief second, she had a flashback of her people on the train when she was traveling to and from Washington to Virginia with the two little White children. She wished that she had 'stood up' for justice like Richard Allen had done.

Bertha was entirely intrigued with learning that the A.M.E. Church, with the founding of its first church, "Mother Bethel" in Philadelphia, Pennsylvania was from its early and humble beginning fully organized and now boasted in the annals of history, twelve colleges and universities – from Wilberforce University, Wilberforce, Ohio, 1856, to Western University, Quindaro, Kansas, 1896, which was closed in 1952 and its students sent to Wilberforce in Ohio.

Bertha thought of how Eliza felt when she learned about Bertha being given the opportunity to experience Black people *en masse* at Howard University. Bertha wondered what Eliza would say and do if she'd known that twelve institutions of higher learning were founded by *Black* people for the practical purposes of educating and enlightening Black students. Bertha arched her back the way her grandmother did when she became overwhelmed with such reflective thoughts.

Bertha once again became an incessant learner; she could not learn enough about her new found church. She listened and read everything that she could get her hands on. Again, she made sure that Earl Junior learned the principles of the church, become involved in activities for young people and in the worship service, and study to learn as much about his new church, both locally and connectionally, as he possibly could learn. Bertha really liked how Earl Junior's eyes would brighten when he or she would share with Earl Allen what either had been involved in at the church or some historical facts about the church: the A.M.E. <u>Christian Recorder</u> was the oldest Black produced newspaper in the world having begun in 1841; that in 1906, Bishop R.C. Ransom gave a fiery speech about John Brown at the 2nd meeting of the Niagara Movement, Harper's Ferry, and that this speech inspired and motivated other Bishops of the Bishop-led A.M.E. Church, thereby giving impetus to the founding of the National Association for the Advancement of Colored People (NAACP). Lastly, Bertha was very excited to share some A.M.E. information about two historical figures whom she'd read about while she was at Howard: W.E.B. Dubois, the first Black Ph.D. from Harvard University, received

Earl Junior
"... well balanced young man..."

his first appointment at Wilberforce University, an A.M.E. institution, and Frederick Douglass, the great abolitionist, attended Metropolitan A.M.E. Church in Washington, D.C. and his funeral service was held there. Bertha was proud to be a Christian and an A.M.E.

As time passed, Bertha and Earl Junior continued their active involvement in First A.M.E. and they continued to learn about their local church. Bertha discovered that First A.M.E. in Seattle was founded in 1886 and was the oldest Black church in the Pacific Northwest to be founded by African-Americans. September 2, 1890, laity members, among them John T. Gayton, bought a large house on Jones Street and converted it to Jones Street Church, transforming a small Sunday school band of people into an active congregation. Rev. L.S. Blakeney was assigned as the church's first minister, and August 31, 1891, the church was incorporated. The congregation continued to grow and in 1912, the original sanctuary was replaced and Jones Street became 14th Avenue. She thought of how all of this was going on one year before she graduated from Howard University. She was pleased to know that Blacks in Seattle were as driven as many of the other Blacks about whom she'd read and heard about when she was at Howard. W.E. B. Dubois, Ida Wells, Mary Church Terrell, Mary McLeod Bethune, John T Gayton, and many, many others locally and nationally.

Bertha learned more about her church and the work that needed to be done in the church and in the local Seattle community. She was heartened and motivated - so much so, that when her responsibilities at the church were no longer filling her days nor meeting her need to do more for her people, she began to find more venues, especially venues that were addressing the numerous social problems in Seattle.

The newly-formed Urban League was an answer to her desire to help. In 1929 - 1930, the Seattle section of the Urban League was formed and immediately began addressing issues like housing, jobs, public accommodations, education, etc., that were deemed important by the community.

In Seattle, like the rest of the cities across the United States, the 1930's were years of the Depression and life was considerably more difficult for the masses of Blacks than it was before the Depression. Many Blacks did not have jobs and those who did have jobs lost them because positions for unskilled laborers and industrial workers were either scarce, discontinued or given to non-Blacks. Many neighborhoods were segregated with living condition less than desirable for Blacks and racism's ugly head was raised in nearly every venue that Blacks confronted. Overall, jobs were scarce and money and resources were very, very tight.

Whenever she wrote to one of her sorors in Delta to share news of her community and her involvement in the city of Seattle, Bertha realized how much she missed the sisterhood she had experienced at Howard University. Bertha thought how wonderful it would be to have an established chapter of Delta Sigma Theta in Seattle, Washington. Bertha began to communicate with Idell Vertner, a member of one of Delta's already established chapters in Oakland, California, Kappa Chapter, and with Virginia Clark Gayton in Seattle, who like Bertha, had been a member of Alpha Chapter while matriculating at Howard University in the early 1920's.

In March 1931, even though Kappa Chapter was in Oakland, under its auspices a Pyramid Club of Delta Sigma Theta Sorority was organized in Seattle to introduce prospective members to the Sorority. The prospective members invited to the Seattle Pyramid Club included Deloris Brooks, Tessie Miller, Jane Chandler, Madge Cayton, and Altoona Jones.

Interestingly enough, Madge Cayton, who received her BA degree from the University of Washington in 1925, was the granddaughter of Hiram Revels (1822 – 1901), the first African American U.S. Senator from Mississippi who won the seat held by the Confederate leader, Jefferson Davis. Susie Revels Cayton, Madge's mother, was the godmother of Virginia Clark Gayton's husband, John Jacob Gayton, who was the son of John T. Gayton who helped to found First A.M.E. Church. For many years, the Caytons lived a very lucrative life on Seattle's fashionable, 'Capitol Hill'. They employed servants, and their newspaper, <u>The Seattle Republican,</u> was popular and financially successful for many years.

On April 17, 1933, Bertha, Virginia Gayton, and Idell Vertner, working with the Western Regional Director of Delta Sigma Theta, Pauline Slater of Los Angeles, California, founded into the sisterhood a new chapter. Alpha Omicron Chapter became the first Black Greek letter sorority in the Pacific Northwest. Deloris Brooks, Madge Cayton, Jane Chandler, and Tessie Miller became Deltas.

Officers were elected: Tessie Miller was elected president and Bertha became vice-president. Deloris Brooks was elected secretary, Idell Vertner, treasurer, and Jane Chandler, historian. A luncheon was held in the home of Deloris Brooks in honor of Pauline Slater, the Western Regional Director. A beautiful charter and a crimson and cream pennant were presented to this new chapter by the regional director. Gladys Byram Shepperd, the National President, added Alpha Omicron Chapter to the growing sisterhood of Delta. Alpha Omicron Chapter began its work in the Seattle community and Bertha Pitts Campbell was ecstatic!

Immediately after Alpha Omicron Chapter was established, two other young women became members of the Chapter's Pyramid Club: Irene Graves and Naomi Tiggs. During the fall of 1933, seven more women joined the Pyramid Club. Delta Sigma Theta in Seattle continued to grow and prosper.

On April 18, 1933, after the founding of Alpha Omicron Chapter, it occurred to Bertha that she'd come full circle in a way. She actually repeated out loud that Virginia Gayton's husband,

John Gayton, was the son of John T. Gayton, a founder of her church, First A.M.E. and Madge Cayton's grandfather, Hiram Revels, was an A.M.E. minister. Now how interesting was that, she thought!

Several events nationwide served as stimuli for change in Delta Sigma Theta both locally and nationally: The Depression years of the 1930's, the kidnapping of the Charles A. Lindbergh baby, the March on Washington to urge a bonus for veterans and the end of Prohibition with the election of Franklin D. Roosevelt as the President of the United States. Also, Billie Holiday was beginning her singing career, Josh Gibson, at nineteen was establishing himself as the best all-round baseball player, Mary McLeod Bethune was being invited to be one of the advisors in President Roosevelt's 'Black Cabinet," and the 21st Amendment for the repeal of Prohibition was being added to the Constitution. In addition, Dr. Carter G. Woodson's, *The Mis-Education of the Negro* was first published in 1933, further catapulting the thinking of the Sorority.

Alpha Omicron Chapter remained motivated. Their foci included actions to support human needs and human rights. Members gave food to the needy and provided funds for milk for children and bedding for hospitals. Also, there remained an emphasis on attainments of high moral standards and high scholastic achievement among Black students and women.

By late 1935, there was sufficient involvement by women in Seattle to form a Ladies' Auxiliary of the Seattle Urban League. Along with Jessie Shields, Salome Riddle, Vivian Spearman and others, Bertha helped to make the many projects of the auxiliary successful. One of the most significant projects involved the well-being of children.

During the 1930's in Seattle, there was the beginning of the systems of parks the city is so famous for today. To the dismay of many of the auxiliary members, the neighborhood children were not utilizing the parks enough. Too many children insisted on continuing to play in the streets and other equally inappropriate and unsafe places. The Ladies' Auxiliary instituted a program called, "Play in the Park." Each lady gathered as many neighborhood children as she could find and took them on outings to the park on a regular basis so that the children would be exposed to a new and more desirable place to play. They achieved their goal – children were kept off the streets.

The Ladies' Auxiliary was a short-lived organization and soon became absorbed by the Urban League, the parent body. Bertha remained an active member of the Seattle Urban League for nearly forty years.

About the same time Bertha became involved in the Seattle Urban League, she joined the Young Women's Christian Association (YWCA). For more than forty years, she continued to give multifaceted service to that organization. Bertha said that if there were any position she did not serve on at the YWCA, she could not recall what it was!

In 1933, Bertha was a member of the Committee of Management and the chairperson of Finance, and by 1935, she had become the chairperson of the Committee of Management, a position she held for two terms. Bertha was selected to represent her Branch at the national convention in 1936, and that year was historically important because she became the first Black voting member of the Board of Directors. Elected to the position of secretary to the Board of Directors in 1938, Bertha continued to serve the YWCA. By 1943, she assumed the position of chairperson of the Committee to Study Interracial Practices in the Seattle Branch. By now, the Branch had grown and a new building was needed.

Bertha worked tirelessly in the 1930's; however, she had no idea that she would be remembered with other Blacks who, too, were making history across the United States. Zora Neale Hurston published her _Jonah's Gourd Vine_ in 1934.   Mary

McLeod Bethune established The National Council of Negro Women in 1935; also in 1935, Dr. Percy Julian, a research chemist, developed a drug used in the treatment of glaucoma and Joe Louis knocked out Primo Carncra at Yankee Stadium in New York. In 1936, Jesse Owens won four gold medals in track and field events at the 1936 Olympics in Berlin, Germany and William Grant Still was the guest conductor of the Los Angeles Symphony Orchestra at the Hollywood Bowl. Given Bertha's love of the train and the train depot, it's imperative to share that The Brotherhood of Sleeping Car Porters became an authentic union under the leadership of Asa Phillip Randolph on October 1, 1937.

Nationally, the worst of times included the Daughters of the American Revolution (DAR) denying Marian Anderson the privilege of singing at Constitution Hall in Washington, DC on February 27, 1939. The DAR had a policy that included White artists only. First-Lady Eleanor Roosevelt resigned her membership from the DAR when Marian Anderson was denied the privilege or opportunity to sing in the Hall. The 1930's were the best of times and the worst of times for Blacks, and Bertha Pitts Campbell was doing her part to make it the best of times for many whom she served.

Locally, the work continued for Bertha. In 1944, a committee was formed to study and plan for the needs of the YWCA. Bertha was a member of this committee. As chairman of Work Group A: Leadership Emphasis in a Little Convention of 1945, Bertha toiled diligently to assure continuous and increased quality in the YWCA.

From 1947 to 1953, Bertha was a member of the City-Wide Personnel Committee. Later she served two terms as a member of the Board of Directors and four terms as chairman of the East Madison Branch. Bertha's service to the YWCA spanned four decades and touched the lives of thousands.

Bertha was a city liaison and during her many years of volunteering, she became acquainted with many refined men and women of all racial groups. In her letters to her friends and sorors in D.C., she often told them about the hard-working women she had met in Seattle. Bertha further shared that one of her proudest moments was lending her cap and gown to Daisy Dawson when Daisy graduated from the University of Washington in 1948. Bertha also highlighted that Daisy Dawson's Delta 'going over' ceremony into the Alpha Omicron Chapter took place in her home. Daisy, like Bertha, was an ardent public servant and Bertha loved this!

Earl Allen was supportive of his wife during all the years that she worked feverishly to help others. If he were not with the Masons working in that brotherhood, he could be found sharing Earl Junior's life, assuring that he would become a well-balanced young man so that Bertha would have more time to help others. As Earl Junior grew older, he added more strength to Bertha's endeavors. The two men in Bertha's life encouraged her to join the Christian Friends for Racial Equality.

Nineteen forty-two signaled the beginning of an era in Bertha's life which extended her labor for others across multiracial lines. World War II had brought to the forefront a *series* of social injustices, the existence which many White Americans denied. Racism and discrimination were shrewdly disguised by those in power in the Seattle area, but were visible and evident to those on the receiving end. People of color individually and collectively were denied the privileges guaranteed to all under the Constitution of the United States of America. They were denied open housing, access to cultural events, entertainment facilities, and even burial space!

Inequities pervaded the very core of life in the greater Seattle area. No sector was left untouched. Eradicating these social injustices and inequities was the basis of the formation of the Christian Friends for Racial Equality – CFRE. This group of multiracial activists recognized the need for unity of purpose and action in seeking and achieving resolutions to problems. They utilized the 'strength in numbers principles' and sought to involve church people to act in order to gain racial justice and parity.

In 1942 and 1943, the CFRE began to examine cases of discrimination in restaurants, hotels, motels, the Red Cross, theaters, and housing projects. Their efforts resulted in many successes. For example, the Red Cross trained one Chinese American and three African Americans as nurses' aides. As the year passed, the Christian Friends for Racial Equality increased its protest against discrimination. Issues such as War Bond sales only to members of one's own racial group, refusal of admission of African Americans to entertainment centers such as roller rinks, police brutality and restrictive covenants were addressed. Whenever progress was achieved, the group commended those people and agencies who responded to their goal of seeking parity for all persons who were denied equity, especially people of color.

The Christian Friends for Racial Equality, by 1946, had become a timely organization which demanded courage and faithfulness in its expanding work. Multifarious cases of discrimination were attacked by this concerned group. The years of 1947 – 1948 were dedicated to the identification and compilation of 250 sets of sixty-four racially restrictive covenants in Seattle property deeds. These were to be placed in the hands of people who desired to remove these undemocratic and restrictive practices.

During this time, the CFRE secured office space in the centrally-located Arcade Building. This achievement was important because due to the make up of the multiracial group, they had encountered untold difficulties in trying to get space in many buildings. Discrimination in real estate was an incessant problem which was addressed by the determined group.

Other issues receiving the attention of the Christian Friends for Racial Equality were housing for University of Washington students, automobile insurance for non-Caucasians and discriminatory practices in Seattle cemeteries. The CFRE attracted increased interest of and participation by other groups who espoused similar positions of insurgency. For six consecutive years, political action against discriminatory practices became an integral part of the group's work. They supported the state law against discrimination in employment and encouraged people of color to obtain training and to apply for jobs. Many years of work were rewarded by the passage of the Financial Responsibility Act which resulted in a change of policy wherein auto insurance companies were required to grant equal treatment to all. Because there was closer collective action for mutual benefit with community agencies, the Christian Friends for Racial Equality experienced phenomenal growth and expansion.

After fifteen years, the Christian Friends for Racial Equality realized that some real progress had been made. There were now laws against discrimination in employment and accommodations. Seattle's public school system began to select staff based on qualifications and not race. The CFRE recognized that even with some progress, they had a long way to go. The monthly meetings held in churches assured the community of a continuous supply of information, as well as provided opportunities for discussions.

The statement of purpose of the Christian Friends for Racial Equality exemplified the high ideals to which Bertha had strived for so many years: "Equality of opportunity for all men of all races...protest by all peaceful means the denial of rights and privileges...develop a public consciousness against religious and racial discrimination...understanding through social acquaintance...unite us all as one people in one democracy." And although Bertha Pitts Campbell knew social problems would always exist, her participation with the Christian Friends for

Pauline S. Hill

Racial Equality allowed her yet another opportunity to render meaningful service to her community.

Bertha was at a peak in her life. As an organizer and a volunteer, she had reached a level of success few could hope to achieve. As life goes, though, the intense fervor at which she had been working for others was soon to be interrupted.

Because the country was again at war (1941 – 45), every hand was needed to help with the war effort. All able-bodied non-working women were to be drafted into the armed services. These women would work either as domestics or at Bremerton, Washington in the shipyards. Bertha was extremely concerned and frightened by the possibility of having to work at either of these jobs. Moreover, she knew there was some validity to the rumors because in World War I, the precedent had been set. While the healthy and able-bodied men were recruited for combat duty, the women and children worked at home in the factories.

Bertha was in a dilemma: on the one hand she loved her country and felt fiercely patriotic. At the same time, she knew that her country and her people could be served best by retaining her independence. Working in the shipyard would not allow her to retain that independence.

Bertha mid 40's

The call came and women who were in the home were asked to fill jobs vacated by men who went off to war. Bertha had discussed this matter of work with her friend, soror, and confidant, Willetta Gayton, who suggested to her that she ask her husband to find out about hiring procedures at the Post Office. When she learned what they were, Bertha, without letting Earl Allen know, studied, took, and passed the required test. Then Bertha interviewed for the job as a postal clerk and was hired to work as an indefinite war substitute.

When Bertha interviewed for the job, without hesitation, she told the interviewer that she could not work the day shift because she was a married woman and mother who had to be at home when her husband and son returned home. She knew from having talked with others that there was a 6 – 10 PM shift which school teachers and other moonlighters were working. She was determined to join this group of workers. Bertha was unyielding with her decision not to work the day shift. She was hired as a clerk and worked the 6 – 10 PM shift for almost three years. When the recruits returned in 1945, Bertha's shift changed and she worked the 3 – 10 PM shift for several more years.

Employment did not stop Bertha's volunteer wheels from turning. As a matter of fact, some of Bertha's most notable achievements came during the 1940's; for instance, her work in the Christian Friends for Racial Equality and the induction of new members like Daisy Dawson into the Sorority.

Early in the war years, Bertha organized a Canteen for African American soldiers at the newly formed Young Men's Christian Association (YMCA). The soldiers were coming into Seattle from Fort Lewis, Washington, and the Canteen offered them a place to rest and relax. Soldiers, especially African American soldiers, were able to enjoy, rest, and recuperate between periods of active duty because of the efforts of Bertha Pitts Campbell. These times in Bertha's life reminded her again of Washington, D.C. Discrimination in Seattle was very widespread even though it was more subtle than in the nation's capital.

The Boeing Company brought numerous young Black women into the Seattle area. Arriving from all parts of the country, they had no place to stay as little housing was available to them. Recognizing the need, Bertha helped to locate lodging for large numbers of these women.

Another notable accomplishment in the 1940's was the founding of Beta Psi Chapter of Delta Sigma Theta Sorority,

Inc. in Portland, Oregon. Originally, there could be no Beta Psi because there were not enough Delta members in Portland to form a chapter. Interested members would have to be inducted into Seattle's Alpha Omicron Chapter. Beta Psi Chapter was founded on March 24, 1945, and they had ten charter members, some of whom were Hattie Gaskins, June Key, Ellen Law and Mignon Lilly Cabell, who was elected president. They noted for their history that the National President was Mae Wright Peck, another sister who fought for justice and equality for women. March 24, 1945 became a time of rejoicing. Members of both Seattle and Portland chapters were glad to find an occasion for celebration because the nation was headed towards a recession, and there was little else about which to feel festive. Amidst it all, Bertha had done it again!

Earl Allen beamed and often teased 'his ol lady' about being as tough as that old iron horse (train) that she admired so much since she was a child. She knew, though, that he was proud of her and her work and whenever she got a chance, she would do something extra special for him to show him just how pleased she was with his support and love.

By 1950, the Post Office requested that Bertha change her status from indefinite war substitute to a permanent position. She refused! She wanted to devote her energies full time to volunteering. More importantly, Earl Allen needed her now that Earl Junior had become a part of the armed forces. Bertha terminated her tenure with the Post Office.

When asked about her retirement benefits, Bertha looked the officer in the eyes and said she would leave the benefits intact until age sixty-two rather than accepting them at that time. Bertha left the Post Office after ten years of service.

9

"Bertha, where is your wedding ring?"

"Do you mean that you've just missed it?"

Bertha confessed to Earl Allen that she had lost her wedding band while washing some clothes. She did not worry that Earl Allen would become angry at her. She just did not tell him because she did not want him to know that she could be so careless with something that she treasured as much as she did her wedding ring!

Earl Allen teased her about not wanting all the men at the post office to know that she was a married woman. Even though he was teasing, he rushed her downtown to the nearest jeweler and bought her a plain gold wedding band that she wore until her death. When he gave her that plain gold wedding band, memories flooded her mind as she clearly saw images of when she first saw and fell in love with him in the depot. She loved him at that moment even more than when she had first met him.

Earl Allen and Bertha lived for the letters that came from Earl Junior. Like all other American parents of servicemen, they were watching the development between South Korea and Communist-ruled North Korea. Feeling that war was inevitable, Bertha and Earl Allen longed and prayed for Earl Junior's safe return.

Pauline S. Hill

Earl Junior in the meantime was making the best of his military tour of duty. From each country, he would send to his mother and father, a little token of love. A surge of silk jackets from China started arriving in the States. Bertha shared that, "All of the recruits were sending these silk jackets home and I did not want one."

Earl Junior obliged and did not send his mother a silk jacket. Using his good taste and what he knew about his parents' desire and taste, he chose for his mother and father, one of the most elegantly hand-carved trunks that he could find in China. Bertha thought it breathtakingly beautiful! She sat long hours studying the artistry and craftsmanship long after Earl Allen had gone to bed. As she caressed the wood, she promised to keep all of her memorabilia of a lifetime in it. Later in life, she thought that trunk should become a part of the national archives of Delta Sigma Theta Sorority, Inc.

10

"No! No! It can't be so! He's been in all kinds of battles; he's experienced a small part of the Korean War; he's only thirty-three years old!! He hasn't had a chance to get married nor have children. We are supposed to be the ones to go first! Not my baby!" These are some of the agonizing thoughts that pounded Bertha's head as she clung to her husband upon learning about the death of Earl Junior. There had been a terribly deafening explosion at Ames Terminal Shipyard in 1951, an explosion from shrapnel that claimed the life of the only son of Earl Allen and Bertha Pitts Campbell while he and others performed the task of cleaning those shrapnel.

Losing Earl Junior (February 8, 1918 – August 24, 1951) was an invincible sorrow for both parents. They could not have gotten through their terrible loss without each other. Bertha knew that she needed more than her poetry to get her through this tragedy. She clung to her husband and prayed like she'd never prayed before for God's grace and His mercy to help her keep her strength and sanity.

Earl Allen kept a close watch on Bertha; he could tell that sometimes her mind would wander, even though she was praying all through the day and night. She was also trying desperately to ease her sorrow by working intensely.

After they buried their only son, Earl Allen began to save every cent that he could! Saving money seemed to have become an obsession with him. He shared with Bertha his travel plans for both of them after his retirement from the United States Immigration and Naturalization Station. Bertha reminded Earl Allen of her retirement money and they tried to relinquish their sorrow with thoughts of those future ventures. "Earl became a tomorrow man and I joined him with the plans."

Could it happen again? Could tragedy and trauma find their way again into the heart of a person who had given so much to humanity everywhere?

Bertha and Earl Campbell

"But he was strong, had worked nearly all his life." He had been married to Bertha for thirty-seven years, supporting her in everything she undertook. He had sat with Earl Junior, reading to him, watching him grow, and meeting him at the depot whenever he came home from the Marines. He'd buried his son and regained the courage to continue on after Earl Junior's death. He had been Bertha's strength through the deaths of her grandmother, her parents, her sister Minnie, her brothers, and many in his family as well. He had been a contributing member of the Herculean Lodge #17, F and AM; Prince Hall Consistory #67; United Supreme Council 33rd degree and last degree; and he had been deputy of Washington State Beni Hassan Temple #64 AEAONMS, Inc.

"How could he have fallen victim to a massive heart attack just three years after Earl Allen's tragic accident? Nineteen hundred fifty-four cannot do this to me!" Bertha anguished.

Yet, 1954 had claimed the life of the final person who meant more to Bertha than life itself.

Friends, Earl's family, and her sisters in Delta, especially Mona H. Bailey who was like a daughter to Bertha, rallied around her and gave her solace, strength and support to go on. She found that she had to pray very often for enduring strength. Her favorite poems and Eliza's songs were her constant companions. As she sought a burial space in the Mt. Pleasant Cemetery on Seattle's Queen Anne Hill, she requested adjoining spaces for she knew that whenever death tracked her down, she wanted to be buried next to her beloved Earl Allen and very close to her dear son, Earl Junior.

*N*ow that Earl Allen (1893 – 1954) was gone, there were so many things that Bertha had to do for herself and to consider. After marrying Earl Allen, she had become dependent on him in so many ways even though she was an independent spirit. As she walked through the home they had shared for so long, she realized that she could not stay there; she could not keep it up alone.

Staring out the window at the car that Earl Allen loved to drive and was now just sitting there looking lonely and missing its driver, Bertha realized that *she* had never learned to drive because Earl Allen or Earl Junior would take her every place she wanted to go. They had spoiled her and now both were gone! At sixty-five years old, what would she do with the car? What would she do with the house? Could she keep that big house all by herself? Could she learn to drive at sixty-five?

Pauline S. Hill

Time passed...

After two attempts, Bertha passed the driving test. She was proud! The house, however, was another story! It became too much for one person, so after two years, she sold it and moved in with a friend, Nella Carter, who lived on South Spokane Street in Seattle's Beacon Hill. Companionship was exactly what she needed, and she found herself talking about things as common as hats. She loved hats, and she talked incessantly about the leghorn hats of long ago that were made of the finest, softest straw. These conversations with Nella were plentiful and satiating, and Bertha enjoyed them immensely, for nearly six years.

Fate intervened tragically once more. Nella died and Bertha was faced with decisions once more!

Her move into the Hilltop Retirement Apartments owned by First Baptist Church in Seattle, left Bertha feeling a little tired and very wary. Even her back ached with pain that often became very intense. She had never before felt physical hurt like that. "I couldn't walk; I was in a wheelchair. Dr. William Womack, a psychiatrist who was a very dear friend of mine, insisted that I check into a hospital after I told him I couldn't put my weight on my left leg.

"I took Billy's advice and in 1962, I checked into the hospital and surgery was prescribed. I left the hospital after a successful operation with only a note of advice from the doctor: 'Put some meat on those bones.' I was nothing but skin and bones."

The Hilltop Retirement Apartment proved a great choice for Bertha!

Too Young to Be Old

Bertha 90's

After 1962, Bertha remained involved in her community and especially with the Seattle Alumnae Chapter of Delta Sigma Theta Sorority, Inc., and other chapters from around the nation and the world. She addressed vast audiences on numerous occasions. Young and old sorors and constituents wanted to be near her, to touch her, to hear her voice, to receive a much sought after autograph, to embrace her. Wherever she appeared, she always drew a crowd because she always had a story to tell.

At the 1978 Delta Sigma Theta Sorority Regional Conference in Portland, Oregon, Portland's Mayor Neil Goldschmidt in the opening session presented to Bertha a copy of <u>Oregon II</u>, an illustrated book which described the scenic areas of Oregon. Bertha graciously accepted the book at the historical conference and later had this to share about Oregon:

"Long time ago, Earl and I needed a room for the night. We drove to a hotel and asked for a room. The hostess kept replying, 'I don't know.'

"I thought to myself, 'She doesn't know what?'

"Finally, the hostess said, 'We don't ordinarily take Negroes in here. You may stay if you promise not to take the blankets when you go.'"

"Earl became furious! 'Dammit, Bertha, we're not going to stay here.'

"Yes we will. We're going to stay right here. I'll see to it that she gets these old blankets back.

"The next morning, I carefully rolled the blankets and said to the hostess, 'Now here are your blankets. We don't want or need them. We have as good blankets at home as these are. Now take your blankets.'"

There was always a story for Bertha to tell, for her experiences were vast!

Saturday, August 23, 1980: Bertha Pitts Campbell was marching down the streets of Seattle, Washington with members and supporters of the Equal Rights Amendment in honor of the Suffragettes. Spring Street – ERA – Seattle – Bertha Pitts Campbell!

August 2, 1981: At age 92, Bertha Pitts Campbell led more than 10,000 sorors of Delta Sigma Theta and their constituents down Pennsylvania Avenue, Washington, D.C to commemorate the Sorority's participation in the March of the Suggragettes in 1913. This time, she was at the front of the March! Even though an antique car was provided to transport her because of distance, she walked the entire length of the march!

In 1981, Bertha said, "There were twenty-two of us who founded Delta in 1913 at Howard University. None of us thought it would grow to what it is today. Only a few of us are left to witness the growth. Nobody is left but Osceola (Soror Founder

Osceola McCarthy Adams of Washington, D.C.), Eliza (Soror Founder Eliza P. Shippen of Washington, D.C.), Winona (Soror Founder Winona Cargile Alexander of Jacksonville, Florida), Naomi (Soror founder Naomi Sewell Richardson of New York), and me.

"I never thought I'd live to get this old. I've outlived all of my relatives except my one niece, Vessie Branson of Los Angeles, California. I'm grateful to God to be alive and of sound mind and good health. I don't know how long I'll live; no one knows. I remember the quip that says, 'The success of living to become one hundred is to get to ninety-nine and then being very careful.'"

Bertha Adine Pitts Campbell lived longer than ninety-nine; she remained active for more than 100 years, leaving this earthly world two months before her 101st birthday (June 30, 1889 – April 2, 1990).

Ellis H. Casson, a noted minister and retired presiding elder of the A.M.E. Church, says at every funeral he preaches that whenever a life is well-lived, his job is really easy because the person would have written his/her own obituary and sermon through works, deeds, and soul redeeming acts. At funerals, therefore, he would only have to reiterate what was done while living. Bertha Pitts Campbell so lived!

A Memorial Service for Bertha Adine Pitts Campbell was held at First A.M.E. Church, Seattle, Washington, April 7, 1990. Local and out of state sorors, friends, and 'dignitaries' paid tribute to one who used collective action and hard work to promote excellence and assistance to those disenfranchised and in need. The Delta choir sang, "Jesus, You're the Center of My Joy."

Pauline S. Hill

The Rev. Vashti Murphy McKenzie, a soror, and who since Soror Campbell's death, has become the first female Bishop of the A.M.E. Church, when preaching Soror Campbell's eulogy, entitled it, 'A Celebration of Life.' We attendees simply had to celebrate this great life because she had 'written her life's work' while she lived.

This author, like many attendees, thanked the good Lord for giving us one who was indeed the center of our joy! Bertha Pitts Campbell was indeed a remarkable, spirited, and giving legend who was *"Too Young to Be Old."*

In a Wednesday, April 11, 1990 <u>Capital Hill Times</u> (Seattle, Washington) article written by columnist Rebecca Jones after Bertha's death, there were several quotes used by Ms. Jones. She stated:

"John Frost, administrator of Hilltop House, where Campbell resided, said, 'I thought she was just an incredible person to have here. She accomplished ideally what one is suppose to accomplish in a life. I've been impressed.'"

Continued Ms. Jones paraphrasing the words of Mona H. Bailey, the 17th National President of Delta Sigma Theta Sorority, "Although Campbell had many laudable achievements, she never wanted to be put on a pedestal and always wanted to be working right along side everybody else."

Lastly, Ms. Jones wrote, "At festivities celebrating her 100th birthday last year, Campbell said she was overwhelmed by the flood of tributes offered in her honor. 'I never knew I could do so much,' she said."

A Delta Sigma Theta Sorority, Inc. Omega Omega Service, a traditional 'last rites' service, was held for Founder Bertha Pitts Campbell. In the printed program was a response by Founder Campbell delivered at the 33rd National Convention of the Sorority held in Seattle in 1975. Soror Founder Campbell wrote:

I wish I could give you Mt. Rainier
But the Folks wouldn't part with it out here.
I wish I could give you the Puget Sound
Or, one of the lakes that is lying around.
I wish I could give you a mild winter's day
Or one of the beaches on which we play.
I wish I could give you the scent of the pine,
Or, the thrill of the trout at the end of your line.
I wish I could give you the Olympics snow-capped
Lying like an accordion in God's lap.
The mountain, the hills, the meadowlark's trills,
The climate that banishes all of your ills,
But these are the gifts of God to give,
So, enjoy Seattle,
and live, live, live ...

Bertha Adine Pitts Campbell rests in a gravesite in the Mount Pleasant Cemetery, 700 West Raye Street, located on the north side of Queen Anne Hill, Seattle, Washington 98119 – 2254, US. On her pyramid shaped headstone, one can read information about her beloved sorority, Delta Sigma Theta, Inc. Resting beside her is her beloved husband, Earl Allen Campbell, Sr., and resting nearby is her beloved son, Earl Allen Campbell, Jr.

A life lived extraordinarily well ~ one which continues to impact generations today and generations yet to come.

Bertha Adine Pitts Campbell

June 30, 1889 - April 2, 1990

A single rose is placed on the gravesite of Bertha Pitts Campbell by the author. Bertha Pitts Campbell is identified as "a black activist" and recognized on the cemetery's list of "notable people" buried at Mount Pleasant Cemetery on Seattle's Queen Anne Hill.

A quick glimpse of some of Bertha Pitts Campbell's life work:

- Co-founded Alpha Chapter, Delta Sigma Theta Sorority, Inc. with 21 other undergraduate students on the campus of Howard University, Washington, D.C, 1913.

- Joined First African Methodist Episcopal Church, Seattle, Washington, late 1920's.

- A founding member of Alpha Omicron Chapter of Delta Sigma Theta, the first Black Greek letter sorority to be established in the Pacific Northwest, Seattle, Washington, April 17, 1933.

- A founding member of Beta Psi Chapter, Delta Sigma Theta Sorority, Inc., Portland, Oregon, 1945.

- Volunteered with the Phyllis Wheatley Branch of the Seattle Young Women's Christian Association (YWCA) for forty years; was the first African American to sit on the Board of the YWCA as a voting member.

- Helped to charter the Christian Friends for Racial Equality, an interracial organization which promoted understanding among racial groups, 1950.

- Assisted with chartering Tacoma Alumnae Chapter, Tacoma, Washington, 1971.

- Assisted with hosting the 33rd National Convention of Delta Sigma Theta Sorority, Inc., held in Seattle, Washington, 1975.

- One of twenty-two (22) sorority members (sorors) who chartered Seattle Alumnae Chapter, Delta Sigma Theta Sorority, Inc. Seattle, WA, September 9, 1979

- Participated in a Seattle march for the Equal Rights Amendment, 1980.

- At age 92, led more than 10,000 sorors of Delta Sigma Theta Sorority, Inc. and their constituents down Pennsylvania Avenue, Washington, D.C. to commemorate the Sorority's participation in the march of the suffragettes in 1913 as well as to highlight the quest for women's rights, August 2, 1981. She refused to ride in the limousine provided for her; she walked the entire route.

- Assisted with chartering the Bellevue Alumnae Chapter, the 800th chapter, Bellevue, Washington, January 28, 1989.

- Received the Metropolitan YWCA "Woman of Achievement Award" December 1989, for services rendered.

- Honored by the Washington State Human Rights Commission as a citizen whose contributions made a difference in the city of Seattle, the state of Washington, and the USA, February 1990.

- Actively supported the Seattle Urban League.

- Bequeathed $6000 to Delta Sigma Theta Sorority, Inc. for a Bertha Pitts Campbell Scholarship Fund in order to support the education of students.

In her book **Calabash: A Guide to the History, Culture & Art of African Americans in Seattle and King County, Washington,** Esther Hall Mumford wrote, "...This assertiveness and advocacy for full participation of African Americans, and later, the elderly, in American life were hallmarks of this quiet woman who graduated valedictorian of her 1908 class at Montrose (Colorado) High School..."

"...always a story to tell..."

Bertha with young Deltas. Bertha was loved and too young, to be old!

Bertha and niece Vessie Branson of Los Angeles, California

"I never thought I'd live to get this old..."

Bertha celebrating her 91st birthday with members of Alpha Omicron Chapter (now Seattle Alumnae Chapter) Seattle, Washington

Bertha has a 100th birthday celebration with members of the Bellevue Alumnae Chapter.

"...Mona was like a daughter to her..."

Bertha escorted into the room by Mona H. Bailey, Delta's 17th National President, and long-time Delta Dorothy Hollingsworth of the Seattle Alumnae Chapter.

Bertha shares a dinner with family and friends at a Seattle restaurant.

References

African American in the Twentieth Century, B. Davis Schwartz Memorial Library: http://www.liu.edu/cwis/cwp/library/african/2000/1930.htm.

"A True Girl-Friend, Nannie Burroughs," The African American Registry: http://www.aaregistry.com/african_american_history/858/A_true_GirlFriend_Nannie_Burroughs_.

Black Oral History Interviews, 1972-1974, Black Studies/ Quintard Taylor. Interviewee: Virginia Gayton: http://www.wsulibs.wsu.edu/holland/masc/finders/cass2.htm.

Calabash: A guide to the History, Culture, and Art of African Americans in Seattle and King County, WA, Esther Hall Mumford, Ananse Press, Seattle, 1993.

HistoryLink.Org. The Online Encyclopedia of Washington State History. "Gayton, John (1899-1969)." HistoryLink.org Essay 397.http://www.historylink.org/essays/output.cfm?file_id=397.

Kansas Historical Society, "Benjamin 'Pap' Singleton: a Kansas Portrait. http://www.kshs.org/portraits/singleton_benjamin.htm.

Mary Church Terrell by Roberta Church and Ronald Walker: http://www.tnstate.edu/library/digital/terrell.htm.

New Perspectives on the West, Benjamin 'Pap' Singleton: http://www.pbs.org/weta/the west/people/s_z/singleton.htm.

Northwest Black Pioneers: A Tribute, 1994, by Ralph Hayes, Washington, and Joe Franklin, Oregon.

The African Methodist Episcopal Church: Know Your Church Manual, Andrew White, The Division of Christian Education, African Methodist Episcopal Church, 1965.

Wikipedia: the free encyclopedia, "Delta Sigma Theta Sorority," http://en.wikipedia.org/wiki/Delta_Sigma_Theta.

Women in History: Mary McLeod Bethune – women@womeninhistoryohio.com, http://www.lkwdpl.org/wihohio/beth-mar.htm.

About the Author

On the sixth day of December, nineteen hundred sixty-three, I was inducted into the Gamma Upsilon Chapter of Delta Sigma Theta Sorority, Inc., Benedict College, Columbia, South Carolina. One part of my intake process was to become acquainted with the twenty-two founders of the Sorority. Written information was researched and oral inquiries made in order to learn about these twenty-two women.

Like many of my sorority sisters, or sorors as they are fondly called, we attended regional conferences and national conventions hoping to meet the surviving founders. We saw them from afar; however, it proved impossible to meet one of them.

In 1975, the Sumter Alumnae Chapter, Sumter, South Carolina selected me, their president, to be the delegate to the thirty-third National Convention in Seattle, Washington. Methodical maneuvering gained me the opportunity to shake the hands of Soror Founder Bertha Pitts Campbell and to get a close-up picture of her.

November 23, 1976, my two children and I moved to Seattle, Washington. Upon learning about the Delta chapter in the area, I joined the Alpha Omicron Chapter. To my unparalleled delight, Soror Founder Bertha Pitts Campbell was an active member of Alpha Omicron and she, like I, missed very few meetings.

As time passed, I wanted to know more about the personal life of my heroine; therefore, I approached my friend and soror, Sherrilyn Johnson Jordan, and we agreed to write a mini-biography on Soror Founder Campbell.

Sherrilyn and I enjoyed interviewing Soror Founder Campbell in her Hilltop House apartment in Seattle. With each meeting, we felt as if we were in an archive as she shared historical memories and memorabilia with a zeal and love that we pass on to our sorors and readers of this work.

Too Young to Be Old: the Story of Bertha Pitts Campbell, was first published in 1981. Over the past few years I have received numerous inquiries about the book, and now, in 2008, I write this Revised Edition of *Too Young to Be Old, the Story of Bertha Pitts Campbell.*

After 40 years in education, I retired July 31, 2006. In Seattle, I served as an education director who supervised one K-8 principal and 20 elementary principals. Prior to that position, I served as principal in Seattle and a teacher in Seattle and South Carolina. I devote many volunteer and leadership hours to community organizations, especially Delta Sigma Theta Sorority, Inc. and my church, First African Methodist Church in Seattle. I am a compassionate Christian, a mother of two grown children, a grandmother of two, and an avid traveler.

Printed in the United States
121970LV00004B/313-1500/P